From Servants to Sons

Mission: To Proclaim Transformation and Truth

Published by: Transformed Publishing

Website: www.transformedpublishing.com

Email: transformedpublishing@gmail.com

Copyright © 2020 by Diana Hicks

All rights reserved solely by the author. No part of this book may be reproduced, stored in a retrieval system, or transmitted in any form or by any means without expressed written permission of the author.

Cover Photography by MR-AH Photography

Scripture is taken from the King James Version ®. Publisher: Public Domain

ISBN: 978-1-953241-07-8
Printed in the U.S.A.

From Servants to Sons

by Diana Hicks

Dedication

- *To my parents:*
  Jimmy & Jessie Hicks

- *To my children:*
  Benson Jr., Darius, Bethany, & Brittany

- *To my grandkids:*
  Kay'Lahni, Rhys, Asiah, & Sevy

- *To my church family:*
  The Apostolic Church of Jesus, New Deliverance Ministries

Table of Contents

Introduction	pg. 1
Chapter 1: Servitude to Sonship	pg. 3
Chapter 2: Benefits of Sonship	pg. 11
Chapter 3: Covenant Rights of Sonship	pg. 17
Chapter 4: And the Word Became Flesh	pg. 21
Chapter 5: Transformation	pg. 31
Chapter 6: Arise	pg. 45
Endnotes	pg. 55
About the Author/ Other Works	pg. 56
Journal	pg. 59

Introduction

In this season God is moving the church from servants to Sons. When I think of servants, the scripture says we are servants to sin. In this teaching I am connecting servants to sin or to the flesh. As long as we are servants, we are still dealing with the flesh. I understand that as long as we are in the flesh, we will have issues with the flesh, but be assured, God wants to establish us and settle us as believers, but it only comes through Sonship.

There are believers dealing with darkness, deep issues, and strongholds in their flesh. However, I am connecting Sonship to the Spirit because when we are led by the Spirit, God gives us the power to become Sons of God. This power enables us to overcome darkness, as stated in John 8:36, "If the Son therefore shall make you free, ye shall be free indeed."

1
Servitude to Sonship

Moving from servitude to Sonship brings forth authority and an inheritance. It brings the Spirit of the Holy Ghost which affords us the opportunity to be in the family of God.

> If we say that we have fellowship with him, and walk in darkness, we lie, and do not the truth: But if we walk in the light, as he is in the light, we have fellowship one with another, and the blood of Jesus Christ his Son cleanseth us from all sin.
> 1 John 1:6-7

Because of the COVID-19 pandemic, a virus that has caused thousands to die, many brick and mortar churches have closed. Because we are not in the four walls, many Christians are backsliding or backing up. God has said to me in my time of prayer to tell the church it is not time for us to slack up, but for the church to stand.

Those that God are allowing to go into the next season must have purpose. In order to have purpose, we must become Sons that fulfil the joy of the Lord. Let me explain because I know most people feel that the bible encourages us to be servants, but there is a level of Sonship God is calling the church to.

> But as many as received him, to them gave he power to become the sons of God, even to them that believe on his name:
>
> John 1:12

Receiving Jesus is more than just reading about Him. It requires us to experience Him, to repent of our sins, and to become acquainted with His griefs through fellowship and suffering.

> That I may know him, and the power of his resurrection, and the fellowship of his sufferings, being made conformable unto his death;
> Philippians 3:10

Believing is more than just getting the knowledge of something. Believing is trusting and confiding in something or someone.

> Trust in the LORD with all thine heart; and lean not unto thine own understanding. In all thy ways acknowledge him, and he shall direct thy paths.
> Proverbs 3:5-6

> There is therefore now no condemnation to them which are in Christ Jesus, who walk not after the flesh, but after the Spirit.
> Romans 8:1

If we are going to become Sons, we must walk in the Spirit and one of the things walking in the Spirit requires is maintaining a prayer life and communication with God. It takes practice to walk in the Spirit. We must practice reading the Word. We must practice praying daily. We must walk not after the flesh, but after the Spirit.

> For the law of the Spirit of life in Christ Jesus hath made me free from the law of sin and death. For what the law could not do, in that it was weak through the flesh, God sending his own Son in the likeness of sinful flesh, and for sin, condemned sin in the flesh: That the righteousness of the law might be fulfilled in us, who walk not after the flesh, but after the Spirit. For they that are after the flesh do mind the things of the flesh; but they that are after the Spirit the things of the Spirit.
> Romans 8:2-5

Remember if we are led by God, we have been given power to become Sons. This is not the time to give up but to push and to establish a real relationship with God. It is time to seek the Lord. To partake of this next season, we must become Sons of God.

In this season God is looking for the fivefold ministry, especially the evangelist. God wants the evangelist to point us in the right direction. That direction is towards Sonship.

As I prepared to write this book, I asked God for two things: to give me the tongue of the learned to be able to speak a Word in season and that God would give this generation the Spirit of the sons of Issachar. The sons of Issachar were men that understood the times. We need to have spiritual understanding of the times.

Again, God said, "Tell my people it's no time to slack up. It's no time to get weary. It's time to become Sons."

Servants only live temporarily in the house and are not permanently in the house. Servants only do what they are told to do or trained to do. However, a Son has authority and is permanently in the house. The Son has security and an inheritance. When he walks this earth, he knows that his Father owns everything. As confirmed in Psalm 24:1, "The earth is the LORD's, and the fulness thereof; the world, and they that dwell therein." Our Lord has given us access because we are Sons of God.

2 Corinthians 5:7 encourages us to operate in faith: "For we walk by faith and not by sight." Through faith as Sons of God, you can walk in your healing, and you can walk in your deliverance because you know who your Father is.

> So then they that are in the flesh cannot please God. But ye are not in the flesh, but in the Spirit, if so be that the Spirit of God dwell in you. Now if any man have not the Spirit of Christ, he is none of his. Romans 8:8-9

I prophesy to you now, "You can't die in this season because you have a work to declare." God has a plan for your life, you are moving into the next season because you are a Son. As a Son, you must fulfill your purpose.

Jesus Christ was our example. The bible says in 1 John 3:8, "...For this purpose the Son of God was manifested, that he might destroy the works of the devil." We too must know our purpose - *that purpose* will fulfill the Joy of the Lord. Confess Psalm 118:17 over your life, "I shall not die, but live, and declare the works of the LORD."

As a Son, you are to fulfill the Father's purpose. Anyone can be a father but when you say Daddy, that declares an endearment. Some Christian literature translates Abba to Daddy, which suggests it is a childlike, intimate term for one's Father.

> For ye have not received the spirit of bondage again to fear; but ye have received the Spirit of adoption, whereby we cry, Abba, Father. The Spirit itself beareth witness with our spirit, that we are the children of God: And if children, then heirs; heirs of God, and joint-heirs with Christ; if so be that we

suffer with him, that we may be also glorified together.

Romans 8:15-17

Directions: Please turn to the Journal beginning on page 59 to respond to these mediation points:

1. Explain what gives you the authority or power to become a Son of God. Read John 1:12.

2. Can you practice walking in darkness and have fellowship with God? Explain. Read 1 John 1:6.

3. Explain the benefits of walking in the light.

4. Explain what it means to receive Christ. Read John 1:12 and Philippians 3:10.

5. Explain how the benefits from your natural father are similar and different than those from your heavenly Father. Read Luke 11:13, Luke 12:29-31, and Psalm 24:1.

6. Explain what connects you with Christ. Read Romans 8:8-9.

7. As believers, how do we receive the inheritance we are entitled to? Read Psalm 2:8.

2
Benefits of Sonship

- **Sonship Brings Glory**
- **Sonship Brings Security**
- **Sonship Brings Faith**
- **Sonship Brings Authority**
- **Sonship Brings the Likeness of Jesus Christ**

> For I reckon that the sufferings of this present time are not worthy to be compared with the glory which shall be revealed in us. For the earnest expectation of the creature waiteth for the manifestation of the sons of God.
> Romans 8:18-19

During Solomon's dedication of the temple through worship, the glory was so great that the ministers could not serve (*see* 1 Kings 8). When the true glory of God shows up there is no service, just worship; we are to walk in our authority. The bible says that when the Son shows up, the glory shall be revealed in us. That glory, which will be revealed in us, is Sonship.

> Now I say, That the heir, as long as he is a child, differeth nothing from a servant, though he be lord of all; But is under tutors and governors until the time appointed of the father. Even so we, when we were children, were in bondage under the elements of the world: But when the fulness of the time was come, God sent forth his Son, made of a woman, made under the law, To redeem them that were under the law, that we might receive the adoption of sons. And because ye are sons, God hath sent forth the Spirit of his Son into your hearts, crying, Abba, Father. Wherefore thou art no more a servant, but a son; and if a son, then an heir of God through Christ.
>
> Galatians 4:1-7

In addition to Glory, Sonship brings security. Sonship brings faith. Sonship brings authority and the likeness of Jesus Christ. There is a likeness on you. When the enemy sees you, he does not see you alone, but he sees the Son.

You have been made righteous through the Blood of Jesus. Therefore, we have a status not of slaves but of Sons. You are not a slave but a Son.

Genesis 22 gives us the account of when Abraham took his son Isaac up to Mt. Moriah to be sacrificed. In verse 7, Isaac asked his father Abraham, "…Behold the fire and the wood: but where is the lamb for a burnt offering?"

Isaac had to become willing to be a sacrifice. Likewise, Jesus Christ became a sacrifice for you and me. In other words, if we are to become Sons we must be willing to become a living sacrifice. The bible says we are to present our bodies a living sacrifice;

holy and acceptable unto God (*see* Romans 12:1).

> [Paul said,] "I am crucified with Christ: nevertheless I live; yet not I, but Christ liveth in me: and the life which I now live in the flesh I live by the faith of the Son of God, who loved me, and gave himself for me.
> Galatians 2:20

Unless you are willing to die, you can't become a Son. Die to the flesh. Die to the old man. Die to your ways.

Abraham's two sons, Ishmael and Isaac, had two different mothers, Hagar and Sarah. One was a servant, and one was permanently in the house. Hagar, who was the servant, was temporarily in the house. She was eventually evicted out of the house because she was a servant (*see* Genesis 21).

When you become a Son, you have perpetual access to the house. You have an inheritance and an authority because you are an heir. An heir has a permanent position secured in the house.

Directions: Please turn to the Journal beginning on page 59 to respond to these mediation points:

1. Explain how suffering with Christ reveals the glory of God in us. Read Romans 8:16-19 and Romans 12:1-2.

2. Explain the security you have as a Son of God. Read Galatians 4:1-7.

3
Covenant Rights of Sonship

You, as a Son, have Covenant Rights of Sonship to declare:

➢ **The promise is unto me and my children.**

For the promise is unto you, and to your children, and to all that are afar off, even as many as the LORD our God shall call.

Acts 2:39

➢ **I am healed by His stripes.**

But he was wounded for our transgressions, he was bruised for our iniquities: the chastisement of our peace was upon him; and with his stripes we are healed.

Isaiah 53:5

> **I can do all things through Christ who strengthens me.**

> I can do all things through Christ which strengtheneth me.
>
> Philippians 4:13

> **A thousand shall fall at my side and ten thousand at my right hand, but it shall not come near me.**

> A thousand shall fall at thy side, and ten thousand at thy right hand; but it shall not come nigh thee.
>
> Psalm 91:7

You have these Covenant Rights because you are a Son. *How do we move from servitude to Sonship?* It is through obedience to God's Word and dying to our flesh.

> Now the Lord is that Spirit: and where the Spirit of the Lord is, there is liberty.
>
> 2 Corinthians 3:17

> … Not by might, nor by power, but by my spirit, saith the LORD of hosts.
>
> Zechariah 4:6

If the Son therefore shall make you free, ye shall be free indeed.
John 8:36

But as many as received him, to them gave he power to become the sons of God, even to them that believe on his name:
John 1:12

You are a Son of God. Stop living beneath your privileges. Sonship makes us free, but servitude represents death. Because we are Sons, we are overcomers. Because we are Sons, we are victorious. Because we are Sons, we have security.

There is a weight of glory God is pouring out on His people, but only upon those who are willing to become Sons. As the songwriter says, "Lord, whatever You're doing in this season, please don't do it without me."[1]

Directions: Please turn to the Journal beginning on page 59 to respond to these mediation points:

1. Explain how you move from servitude to Sonship. Read John 8:35-36 and Zechariah 4:6.

2. Explain the benefits of being in the house. Read Psalm 84:10.

4
And the Word Became Flesh

- Who is Jesus?
- Who is the One we are to become joint heirs with?

I love the book of John because instead of beginning with genealogies, it begins with Jesus.

> In the beginning was the Word, and the Word was with God, and the Word was God.
>
> John 1:1

Not only did John understand the importance of who Jesus was, but he knew who Jesus *really* was. John said the Word was with God, but he takes it a little further and says, *the Word was God.*

> The same was in the beginning with God. All things were made by him; and without him was not any thing made that was made.
>
> John 1:2-3

The Word is God and everything that was made was made by Him (the Word). There should be no confusion about who the Word was and is. The Word was God. The Word is God.

> In him was life; and the life was the light of men. And the light shineth in darkness; and the darkness comprehended it not.
>
> John 1:4-5

This same Word was in the beginning. This means when God said, "Let there be light," in Genesis 1:3, the Word was there speaking the world into existence. To reemphasize, according to these verses we are looking at here in St. John, the Word is God.

> And the Word was made flesh, and dwelt among us, (and we beheld his glory, the glory as of the only begotten of the Father,) full of grace and truth.
> John 1:14

So, we know who John is speaking of when he says the Word was made flesh. John is speaking of Jesus Christ because He is the only begotten of the Father and He brought grace and truth. In other words, Jesus is the same God from the beginning that said, "Let there be light", and the light appeared.

Jesus is God in the flesh. He was God in creation. He was the Son in redemption. He is the Holy Ghost that dwells in us today. He is the only true and living God. The only One that was made flesh was Jesus Christ. We beheld His glory. The disciples saw Him walk the earth in the flesh.

> And without controversy great is the mystery of godliness: God was manifest in the flesh, justified in the Spirit, seen of angels, preached unto the Gentiles, believed on in the world, received up into glory.
>
> 1 Timothy 3:16

This scripture also tells us who Jesus was. He was God manifested in the flesh, coming to redeem man back unto Himself.

> And she shall bring forth a son, and thou shalt call his name JESUS: for he shall save his people from their sins.
>
> Matthew 1:21

Yes, *Jesus shall save His people from their sins!* The only way we can *already* be His people, is that he was God in the flesh. Everyone does not get this mystery. There are not three in heaven, there is only *One*. In Mark 12:29, Jesus declared the same words proclaimed in Deuteronomy 6:4, "And Jesus answered him, The first of all the commandments is, Hear, O Israel; The Lord our God is one Lord:"

> That they all may be one; as thou, Father, art in me, and I in thee, that they also may be one in us: that the world may believe that thou hast sent me.
>
> John 17:21

Yes, understanding Sonship gives you access to the promises of God, but ultimately, God wants us to make disciples and believers in Jesus Christ.

In Matthew 5:16, Jesus instructs us to, "Let your light so shine before men, that they may see your good works, and glorify your Father which is in heaven." We must arise into Sonship. We are joint heirs with Christ. Jesus is the image of the invisible God. God is a Spirit and they that worship Him must worship Him in Spirit and in truth.

> And if ye be Christ's, then are ye Abraham's seed, and heirs according to the promise.
>
> Galatians 3:29

> Who is the image of the invisible God, the firstborn of every creature:
>
> Colossians 1:15

> God is a Spirit: and they that worship him must worship him in spirit and in truth.
>
> John 4:24

To say that you are a Son of God is a powerful point. Jesus is the Word. *Why is all this important?* Because now God wants you and I to become the walking Word. When people see us, God wants them to see the manifestation of his Son which is the Word in us.

> If ye abide in me, and my words abide in you, ye shall ask what ye will, and it shall be done unto you.
>
> John 15:7

We are to become one with His Word through faith. The anointing comes through application. We have to apply this Word to our everyday life in order for the Word to be manifested. In other words, we have to live His Word. When people see us, they ought to see the manifestation of the scriptures:

> No weapon that is formed against thee shall prosper; and every tongue that shall rise against thee in judgment thou shalt condemn. This is the heritage of the servants of the LORD, and their righteousness is of me, saith the LORD.
> Isaiah 54:17

> I can do all things through Christ which strengtheneth me.
> Philippians 4:13

> Who his own self bare our sins in his own body on the tree, that we, being dead to sins, should live unto righteousness: by whose stripes ye were healed.
> 1 Peter 2:24

This is the Word of God. These things may not happen overnight, but as you continue to speak the Word and understand *who* you are and *whose* you are, your faith will increase. Then you, as well as the people around you, will see the manifestation of God's Word in your everyday life. This is why it is so important to God that the church become one and work in unity.

> Now I beseech you, brethren, by the name of our Lord Jesus Christ, that ye all speak the same thing, and that there be no divisions among you; but that ye be perfectly joined together in the same mind and in the same judgment.
> 1 Corinthians 1:10

> Fulfil ye my joy, that ye be likeminded, having the same love, being of one accord, of one mind.
> Philippians 2:2

> For we wrestle not against flesh and blood, but against principalities, against powers, against the rulers of the darkness of this world, against spiritual wickedness in high places.
> Ephesians 6:12

We are to be of one mind, united in thought and purpose. We are not to wrestle against our brother or sister in Christ but against the works of darkness and spiritual wickedness in high places. God wants us to become one as believers with His Word so that the world might believe on Him.

> Now then we are ambassadors for Christ, as though God did beseech you by us: we pray you in Christ's stead, be ye reconciled to God.
> 2 Corinthians 5:20

Directions: Please turn to the Journal beginning on page 59 to respond to these mediation points:

1. Explain why it is important to God to reveal and proclaim oneness. Read John 17:21.

2. Read Galatians 3:29 and explain what it means to you.

3. Explain who is the image of the invisible God and the firstborn of every creature. Read Colossians 1:15.

4. Explain how you become the Word of God and what the benefits are thereof. Read John 15:7.

5
Transformation

- **Salvation**

  That if thou shalt confess with thy mouth the Lord Jesus, and shalt believe in thine heart that God hath raised him from the dead, thou shalt be saved. For with the heart man believeth unto righteousness; and with the mouth confession is made unto salvation. For the scripture saith, Whosoever believeth on him shall not be ashamed.
  Romans 10:9-11

After we receive Jesus Christ as our Lord and Savior through believing on the finished work of the cross; confessing with our mouth and believing in our hearts that God raised Jesus from the dead, we become *saved* and are filled with the power of the Holy Ghost. We must connect with a bible believing church, as well as, read the bible daily and apply it to our everyday life. The Word of God can and will transform you into a Son of God (the walking Word).

The Word of God will renew your mind and that renewed mind will increase your faith to understand that every promise in God's Word is for you as a joint heir with Christ. As we continue on this journey of Sonship, there is perpetual transformation that will take place in your life. Continually confess the Word of God to renew your mind.

> And be not conformed to this world: but be ye transformed by the renewing of your mind, that ye may prove what is that good, and acceptable, and perfect, will of God.
> Romans 12:2

> And if children, then heirs; heirs of God, and joint-heirs with Christ; if so be that we suffer with him, that we may be also glorified together.
> Romans 8:17

➤ The Promises of God are Yea and Amen

> For we would not, brethren, have you ignorant of our trouble which came to us in Asia, that we were pressed out of measure, above strength, insomuch that we despaired even of life:
> 2 Corinthians 1:8

> For all the promises of God in him are yea, and in him Amen, unto the glory of God by us.
> 2 Corinthians 1:20

Paul reveals some of his greatest tests that took place in Asia. Paul felt close to death. The trials and tribulations he faced pushed him to the point that he desired to die. Sometimes situations can change us and change our thinking. Paul speaks of sufferings, afflictions, and being pressed beyond measure, but in 2 Corinthians 1:20, God renews Paul's Spirit through the revelation that all of God's promises toward him are yea and Amen. Everything God has promised you; He will bring it to pass. God keeps His promises.

Another example is John the Baptist. He had firsthand experiences with Jesus, but also felt overwhelmed.

From the womb:

> For he shall be great in the sight of the Lord, and shall drink neither wine nor strong drink; and he shall be filled with the Holy Ghost, even from his mother's womb.
>
> Luke 1:15

In ministry:

> In those days came John the Baptist, preaching in the wilderness of Judaea, And saying, Repent ye: for the kingdom of heaven is at hand. For this is he that was spoken of by the prophet Esaias, saying, The voice of one crying in the wilderness, Prepare ye the way of the Lord, make his paths straight.
>
> Matthew 3:1-3

And preached, saying, There cometh one mightier than I after me, the latchet of whose shoes I am not worthy to stoop down and unloose.

Mark 1:7

He must increase, but I must decrease.
John 3:30

Somewhere along the way, life struggles and trials caused John the Baptist to question the deity of God by sending his disciples to ask the Christ in Matthew 11:3, "…Art thou he that should come, or do we look for another?"

Regardless of the hand life has dealt you, regardless of the test and trials you may face, God is sure of His Word, and He keeps His promises.

I will worship toward thy holy temple, and praise thy name for thy lovingkindness and for thy truth: for thou hast magnified thy word above all thy name.

Psalm 138:2

Diana Hicks

The Word is placed above His name. Therefore, the promises of God in your life are yea and Amen.

➢ **God's Word is His Promise**

> O foolish Galatians, who hath bewitched you, that ye should not obey the truth, before whose eyes Jesus Christ hath been evidently set forth, crucified among you? This only would I learn of you, Received ye the Spirit by the works of the law, or by the hearing of faith? Are ye so foolish? having begun in the Spirit, are ye now made perfect by the flesh?
>
> Galatians 3:1-3

God's Word is His Promise. He has given us an unlimited amount of promises, but the devil wants us to doubt His Word because of what we are going through. Paul address the Galatians as foolish because they once believed God, they once trusted in God through faith, they walked in the Spirit and were believing the preaching of the Word of

God through Paul, yet suddenly, they began to listen to the teachings of the law and the teachings on circumcision. The Galatians began to seek for something else, no doubt because they were going through times of testing and were looking for any way out.

As I write this book, the world is in the midst of a global pandemic. The Coronavirus (COVID-19), has hit the entire world and millions of people have died. People are looking for a way out. Churches and schools have closed. People are turning to other things rather than God, just as they did in Galatia. The Galatians began to turn to other teachings, therefore, Paul addressed them as *foolish* and asked them, "Who has bewitched you that ye should not obey the truth?"

This is not the time to shift or to seek other teachings, this is the time to know that God's promises are yea and Amen. Paul reminds them that they did not receive the Spirit by the works of the law, but by the hearing of faith.

> Wherefore the law was our schoolmaster to bring us unto Christ, that we might be justified by faith. But after that faith is come, we are no longer under a schoolmaster. For ye are all the children of God by faith in Christ Jesus.
> Galatians 3:24-26

The law was a schoolmaster. God used Moses to write the law to make man mindful or conscious of their sins. He wanted them to be aware of their sins and come to the realization they needed something to cleanse their conscience, not just their flesh. We all are subject to the law without Christ. As a schoolmaster, the law reminds us that we need something aside from the law. We need something more because the law alone *didn't* and *doesn't* work.

> For what the law could not do, in that it was weak through the flesh, God sending his own Son in the likeness of sinful flesh, and for sin, condemned sin in the flesh:
> Romans 8:3

For as many as are of the works of the law are under the curse: for it is written, Cursed is every one that continueth not in all things which are written in the book of the law to do them.

> Galatians 3:10

For whosoever shall keep the whole law, and yet offend in one point, he is guilty of all.

> James 2:10

Moses recorded over six hundred laws. If a person broke one, they were guilty of them all. Henceforth, we see the law was not complete because no one could obey all of those commands. Every year the priest had to go before God for the people. If he were not right in the eyes of God, he would be killed in the Holy of Holies, which was the innermost sacred place of the temple, therefore, something else was needed.

We needed another means of hope because the law had no power. That hope is Jesus Christ. Jesus Christ did not come to do away with the law but to fulfil the law. Jesus

Himself said in Matthew 5:17, "Think not that I am come to destroy the law, or the prophets: I am not come to destroy, but to fulfil." See, no man is justified by the law in the sight of God.

➢ The Just Must Live by Faith

> But that no man is justified by the law in the sight of God, it is evident: for, The just shall live by faith. And the law is not of faith: but, The man that doeth them shall live in them. Christ hath redeemed us from the curse of the law, being made a curse for us: for it is written, Cursed is every one that hangeth on a tree: That the blessing of Abraham might come on the Gentiles through Jesus Christ; that we might receive the promise of the Spirit through faith.
>
> Galatians 3:11-14

The just shall live by faith. Christ has redeemed us from the curse of the law. Therefore, our faith is in Jesus Christ. We must believe in the finished work of the cross of Calvary. Declare:

- ✓ By faith I've been delivered.
- ✓ By faith I've received the Spirit of God.

Notice that we are connected with the blessings of Abraham and not the laws of Moses. God told Abraham, in Genesis 12:2, "And I will make of thee a great nation, and I will bless thee, and make thy name great; and thou shalt be a blessing:"

Jesus Christ is the seed of promise and we are the seeds of Jesus Christ. Every promise God has made in the scriptures are for you and me.

It is only when someone dies that the Last Will and Testament comes into effect. When Jesus Christ died on the cross of Calvary, every promise written in the scriptures, was made now unto us. By faith you must believe it.

The bible talks about the difference between the promise of the law and the promise of the gospel. John 1:17 tells us, "For the law was given by Moses, but grace and truth came by Jesus Christ."

You and I were once far from God but have now been brought near by the Blood of Jesus Christ, meaning we were engrafted in and are now the Sons of God or Sons of promise. We can cry Abba Father. Every Son has been given a promise and an inheritance. Remember 2 Corinthians 1:20, "For all the promises of God in him are yea, and in him Amen, unto the glory of God by us."

> And this I say, that the covenant, that was confirmed before of God in Christ, the law, which was four hundred and thirty years after, cannot disannul, that it should make the promise of none effect.
>
> Galatians 3:17

Although the law came after the promises God made to Abraham, it cannot do away with the promises God made to Abraham which are connected to us. Therefore, the law cannot stop the promises God made to you once you receive Jesus Christ as your Lord and Savior. Abraham was made righteous through his belief and faith in God.

> He staggered not at the promise of God through unbelief; but was strong in faith, giving glory to God; And being fully persuaded that, what he had promised, he was able also to perform.
> Romans 4:20-21

We today are made righteous through faith in Jesus Christ. Although we face trials and difficulties in life we must remember that through it all, because we are Sons of God and were made righteous through Christ, every promise of God to you and I are yea and Amen. If God spoke it, He will make it good.

The bible says before one jot or tittle of God's word shall fail, heaven and earth will pass away; all of His promises must be fulfilled.

Diana Hicks

For verily I say unto you, Till heaven and earth pass, one jot or one tittle shall in no wise pass from the law, till all be fulfilled.

Matthew 5:18

Directions: Please turn to the Journal beginning on page 59 to respond to these mediation points:

1. Explain what transforms you and how you can transform your mind. Read Romans 12:1-2.

2. Explain how your purpose is connected to God. Read Philippians 2:13.

3. Explain how your tests and trials have changed you.

4. What promises in the Word of God have helped sustain you during your most difficult times?

5. Explain what fulfilled the law of Moses in the New Testament. Read Romans 8:3.

6. How are you connected to the promises of Abraham? Read Galatians 3:11-14, & 17.

6
Arise

I was impacted by a story I heard Bishop T.D. Jakes[2] tell that I would like to share with you.

A woman received a document from her employer who had recently died. The woman hung the document on her wall as a memorial to the person she had worked with for so many years. One day, a man came to visit this woman's house and noticed the document. She was very poor and had great needs. The man read the document and discovered that it was the Last Will and Testament of her long-time employer who had died. It was proclaimed in this Last Will and Testament, that the woman had been left a house, a car, finances, etc. She had an inheritance of everything she desired and needed, but she was living poor. The reason the Will was on the wall and not cashed out, was because she could not read.

Many times, we are like that woman and living beneath our privileges because we have not read the Will. Our Will is the Word of God - the testaments. You must know God's promises if you are going to receive them. Let's look at a few of God's promises towards us:

- **You are the head, and not the tail.**
- **You are above only, and not beneath.**
- **You have already been forgiven, already have peace, and already are healed.**
- **Your children are blessed, filled with the Spirit of God, and shall prophesy.**
- **You will not die, but live, and declare the works of the Lord.**
- **Whatsoever you ask in prayer believing you will receive.**

And the LORD shall make thee the head, and not the tail; and thou shalt be above only, and thou shalt not be beneath; if that thou hearken unto the commandments of the LORD thy God, which I command thee this day, to observe and to do them:

> Deuteronomy 28:13

But he was wounded for our transgressions, he was bruised for our iniquities: the chastisement of our peace was upon him; and with his stripes we are healed.

> Isaiah 53:5

And it shall come to pass afterward, that I will pour out my spirit upon all flesh; and your sons and your daughters shall prophesy, your old men shall dream dreams, your young men shall see visions:

> Joel 2:28

I shall not die, but live, and declare the works of the LORD.

> Psalm 118:17

Diana Hicks

> And all things, whatsoever ye shall ask in prayer, believing, ye shall receive.
> Matthew 21:22

Those are just a few of God's unlimited promises. You have to read the promises. You have to hear the promises. You have to say the promises. The bible reinforces this truth in Romans 10:17, "So then faith cometh by hearing, and hearing by the word of God." You've got to hear it and speak it over your life.

> How then shall they call on him in whom they have not believed? and how shall they believe in him of whom they have not heard? and how shall they hear without a preacher? And how shall they preach, except they be sent? as it is written, How beautiful are the feet of them that preach the gospel of peace, and bring glad tidings of good things!
> Romans 10:14-15

Remember, the scripture says, God magnifies His Word above His name.

> I will worship toward thy holy temple, and praise thy name for thy lovingkindness and for thy truth: for thou hast magnified thy word above all thy name.
>
> Psalm 138:2

The first Messianic Promise was made in the first book of the Bible.

> And I will put enmity between thee and the woman, and between thy seed and her seed; it shall bruise thy head, and thou shalt bruise his heel.
>
> Genesis 3:15

Here God promises that He will destroy the works of the devil. In other words, this verse points us to the gospel, which is the death, burial, resurrection, and second coming of Jesus Christ. Everything from here points to Christ.

Diana Hicks

Satan influenced man to eat of the forbidden fruit. As a result, all mankind has been born in sin and shapened in iniquity.

> For as in Adam all die, even so in Christ shall all be made alive.
> 1 Corinthians 15:22

> For if by one man's offence death reigned by one; much more they which receive abundance of grace and of the gift of righteousness shall reign in life by one, Jesus Christ.
> Romans 5:17

God had to send his Son in order to redeem man back unto Him. Jesus came to save His people from their sins.

> And she shall bring forth a son, and thou shalt call his name JESUS: for he shall save his people from their sins.
> Matthew 1:21

> He that committeth sin is of the devil; for the devil sinneth from the beginning. For this purpose the Son of

God was manifested, that he might destroy the works of the devil.
                                1 John 3:8

For the devil sinneth from the beginning, refers back to Genesis chapter 3, when the serpent persuaded Adam and Eve to eat of the forbidden fruit. Therefore, *for this purpose, the Son of God was manifested, that He might destroy the works of the devil.* In Genesis 3:15, it was promised that He was coming to bruise the devil's head and in 1 John 3:8, He shows up. God keeps His promises!

For example, if we promise our child a bicycle, that child will keep reminding us of that promise, "Mom, you promised me a bike!" Sooner than later, we will make good on our promise because we are good parents, and we want to do what we have promised.

Well, how much more does our heavenly Father want to, and is willing to, give us what He has already promised. But we have to know what the Word says about us. We have to read the document, then remind God of His promises. As a Son, we must not live beneath our privileges; we must walk by faith and not by sight because God has given us great and precious promises.

> If ye abide in me, and my words abide in you, ye shall ask what ye will, and it shall be done unto you.
>
> John 15:7

> But seek ye first the kingdom of God, and his righteousness; and all these things shall be added unto you.
>
> Matthew 6:33

> Even when we were dead in sins, hath quickened us together with Christ, (by grace ye are saved;) And hath raised us up together, and made us sit together in heavenly places in Christ Jesus:
>
> Ephesians 2:5-6

You are joint heirs with Christ and have been given the authority to sit in heavenly places because of the finished work of the cross of Calvary. Because of whose you are, you can speak God's promises over your life. Write them out and post them on your refrigerator. Post them on your bathroom mirror so that you can see and speak them daily. If you need healing for your body then write out scriptures on healing, post them around your home, workplace, and car so you can read them daily. You can do the same, when you need financial breakthrough, or are praying for the salvation of your child, or the restoration of your marriage. Whatever you are praying for is in the Word of God and God has made you a promise concerning your issue.

> But ye shall receive power, after that the Holy Ghost is come upon you: and ye shall be witnesses unto me both in Jerusalem, and in all Judaea, and in Samaria, and unto the uttermost part of the earth.
> Acts 1:8

It is *that* Holy Ghost power that has given you the authority and the right to become a Son of God.

But as many as received him, to them gave he power to become the sons of God, even to them that believe on his name:

John 1:12

Never forget, Sonship gives you access to all of the precious promises of God.

<u>Directions:</u> Please turn to the Journal beginning on page 59 to respond to these mediation points:

1. Explain why the Son of God was manifested. Read 1 John 3:8.

Endnotes

[1] *Don't Do It Without Me* by Bishop Paul S. Morton

[2] https://www.tdjakes.org/

About the Author

Pastor Diana Hicks was born in Detroit, Michigan to the parents of Jimmy and Jessie Hicks. Pastor Hicks is a native of Riviera Beach, Florida. She attended public schools in Palm Beach County, Florida where she received her High School Diploma at Suncoast Community High School in Riviera Beach. She later continued her education and received an A.A. Degree in Business and a Bachelor's Degree in Education from the University of Central Florida. She has four beautiful children: two girls and two boys.

Pastor Hicks was saved and filled with the Holy Ghost in December 1988 and continued to work faithfully in the church until the true call of God was manifested in her life. She began ministering the Word of God in 1994. Pastor Hicks later became the National Sunday School Superintendent for The Apostolic Church of Jesus, Inc.

Pastor Diana Hicks is a co-recording artist with her brother Bishop Jimmy Hicks and the Voices of Integrity. Their hit records are available on all digital music outlets. Search The Gospel Mix 11 w/ Kerry Douglas on Blacksmoke Music Label, for their latest release *Keep Running.* Other hit releases are:

What You Need God's Got It
Move
Born Blessed
Blessed Like That

God is yet developing and ever-increasing the anointing and call upon Pastor Hicks' life day by day. She is now the Senior Pastor of the Apostolic Church of Jesus, New Deliverance Ministries in Cocoa, FL. She has seen God work many miracles and do miraculous things through-out her ministry.

Please contact Pastor Hicks by email at dianahicks155@gmail.com for ministry engagements and book readings. For bulk book order discount inquiries, please email transformedpublishing@gmail.com.

From Servants to Sons

Journal:

Write Unto the Lord

The Promises of Sonship Must be Your Reality

www.ingramcontent.com/pod-product-compliance
Lightning Source LLC
Chambersburg PA
CBHW071507070526
44578CB00001B/469